MIDDLE SCHOOL
HIGH SCHOOL
COLLEGE & BEYOND

Carole Marsh's CAREERS CURRICULUM™

Would YOU HIRE this PERSON?

A Look at Getting Hired (or not!)...from the Point of View of Your (Possible!) Future Employer

CAROLE MARSH

You know it's not easy to get a job...but have you thought about all these things?! Real-world interview scenarios... and you get to decide the job candidate's fate!

Editor:	Janice Baker
Assistant Editors:	Charles Peterson
	Madeline Vogler
	Adrianna Atkinson
Cover Design:	Lisa Kelly
Content Design:	Randolyn Friedlander
	Lisa Kelly
	Maggie Bowers
Project Manager:	Paige Muh

For additional information about **Carole Marsh's Careers Curriculum** or if you would like permission to use these interview scripts for in-school broadcasting, contact:

Gallopade International
P.O. Box 2779
Peachtree City, Georgia 30269
800-536-2438, ext. 11
www.careerscurriculum.com
www.gallopade.com

Carole Marsh's CAREERS CURRICULUM™

Books

Essential Skills for the Real World of Work: Things *Every* Student Must Know!

Job Tracks: 60* Great Careers—and How to Get from Where You Are...to Where You Want to Go! *Real Job Success Stories from 21st Century Career Pathways!

Would *You* Hire This Person?: A Look at Getting Hired (or Not!)... from the Point of View of Your (Possible!) Future Employer

The Parent and Teacher's Guide to Helping Students Navigate the Bumpy Road from School to More School, First Job, and Career

Business Ethics and Etiquette for Students—You MUST Know These!

WORK WORDS: Job/Business/Career Words and Terms You Need to Know!

Also available in ebook formats

Successful and unsuccessful people do not vary greatly in their abilities. They vary in their desires to reach their potential.

—John Maxwell

Contents

A Word from the Author.................page 7
Will Nerves Undo Her?.................page 9
Ignorance Is No Excuse!.................page 15
Be a Positive, Not a Negative!.................page 21
Better Late Than Never...Or Not?.................page 27
Show Me the Money-Not!.................page 33
Will a Lack of Schooling Hurt Him?.................page 39
What Does Your Body Language Say About You?.................page 45
Think Before You Speak!.................page 51
Control Your Inner "Control Freak!".................page 57
Can You Learn from Your Mistakes?.................page 63
Be Yourself-Not Self-Conscious!.................page 69
The "Name" of the Game.................page 75
Tips to ACE Your Next Job Interview.................page 81

Opportunity is missed by most people because it is dressed in overalls and looks like work.

—Thomas Edison

A Word from the Author

What is a job interview anyway?
It feels like a stress test, doesn't it?
Nothing quite prepares you for a job interview.
It's just hard to think that this person sitting before you holds your employment fate in his or her hands.
Were they ever in your shoes? YES! Were they ever nervous? YES!
Did they make interview mistakes? YES!

My point is...relax.
No one ever aces every interview.
It's a little like performing...practice helps.

No one ever gets a "You're hired!" on every job interview.
Not everyone gets that all important second interview.
Lots of people get a "Thanks, but no thanks, sorry" rejection.

REJECTION...none of us like that. We probably spent our entire middle and high school years trying hard NOT to get rejected. But you know, you can make NO your friend!

If you're trying to build job skills and experience, it starts with the job interview, and, often, with rejection. Since rejection's part of life, it's character-building to figure out how you will respond to the word NO.

Here are some tips:

- Don't take it so personally; you weren't the only one who didn't get the job, you know!
- Embrace adversity: think of how you can prepare and do better the next time.
- Be resilient: you can stay down, but why? Bounce right back up and try again.
- Be confident: many of the most famous and successful and talented people were rejected MANY TIMES; it just goes with the territory.
- Retain your inner belief that you will succeed...and you will!
- Listen to your inner voice: maybe that job really wasn't for you; what if you got it when another, even better, job is waiting in the wings?

Failure and rejection are part of success. As a writer, I eat rejection for lunch! Just tell me NO and I will try harder, be better, and achieve; no one can stop me. Nor you. Embarrassed by rejection letters? Many famous writers proudly wallpapered their offices with them (so they could later gloat over the folks who missed out on their talent)!

Collect your rejections proudly so that when you get a "YES! YOU GOT THE JOB!", you will appreciate it—and yourself—more than ever. Remember: every no is one step closer to a yes...really!

Cheering you on!

Carole Marsh

Whenever it is possible, a boy should choose some occupation which he should do even if he did not need the money.

—William Lyon Phelps

Will Nerves Undo Her?

Nerves are always a factor in a job interview.

Will this job candidate be able to control hers...or will she fall apart at the seams?

Will the interviewer help tame her jitters, or actually egg them on?

Will she hire this person?

Would you?

Meet Jocolyn Metters, recruiter for Chadaroos Insurance, a global firm that insures high-rolling international firms against all eventualities, including tsunamis, terrorism, and just about everything else. She is seeking a strong candidate for a rather basic entry-level position in sales.

Meet Catherine King. Cat, as she goes by, is a nice girl, makes good grades, and is probably a great candidate for the job, but she knows that she always has a problem with nerves keeping her from presenting herself in the best light. She hopes that, over time, she can overcome her fears, but last night, she bit off all her fingernails because she was so nervous about her interview today.

The Interview

Ms. Metters: "Hello, nice to meet you. I am Jocolyn Metters. You must be Cat."

Cat: "Hi! Yes, I'm Cat King. It's nice to meet you as well! I've been looking forward to it."

Heart racing, very hot, concentrate, don't trip, you'll be fine, Cat. Just breathe…

Cat walks quickly and takes a seat, almost tripping in her effort to make it across the room…your first interview can be the most nerve-wracking.

Ms. Metters: "I have reviewed your resume and am impressed with your academics, but do you have any professional experience outside of the school environment? Have you ever done any cold-calling, customer service, or anything pertaining to sales?"

I'm afraid I already know the answer…but maybe she'll surprise me…for the better.

Cat: "Unfortunately, I don't have any professional experience. My focus, until now, has been on school and my part-time job. I was never able to fit an internship into my schedule."

Did I word that wrong? I think I did. Why am I second-guessing myself so much? Just breathe. Be yourself.

Ms. Metters: "Hmmmm. I understand the struggle in finding balance. Hopefully with age you will be able to better prioritize."

Pssshhhh, in this job market, I can find someone equally knowledgeable who also has some experience under their belt. This interview was officially a waste of time; she chose a job over an internship so she could have spending money while in school. We need a professional, not a grown child…

I hope that wasn't a jab. OK, talk…be assertive and confident.

Cat: "I know I lack professional experience, but it was my privilege and responsibility to put myself through school, which actually taught me how to budget my finances and manage my time. And although I don't have experience in an office, I often took charge of term projects in school. For one class, I had to assemble a 63-page research paper on Chicago's apartment zoning. And if it wasn't hard enough getting three writers to sound like one, we also had a comprehensive oral presentation with a Q&A from staff members auditing the presentations. And that was just for one class!"

Goodness! Where did that come from?! Whoa, I talked way too much. She didn't want to hear all that. Ramble ramble ramble. I'm even rambling in my head!! Ah, it feels like it's 101 degrees in here! Please talk! What if I offended her? Oh great, way to go, Cat!

This girl stands up for herself. A little aggressive and "talky" but that isn't such a bad thing to have in sales. OK, I'll bite.

Ms. Metters: "Well, it is admirable that you put yourself through school while maintaining a 4.0 GPA. Were you involved in any extracurricular activities, sporting teams, sorority, anything like that?"

OK, calm down, Cat. She is still keeping eye contact with you.

Cat: "Well…actually I have been volunteering with an organization that helps kids with cleft palates for the past five years or so. Once I organized a community water balloon fight as a fundraiser. It was a pretty sweet gig to coordinate."

Sweet gig—where did that come from!? Not professional, not at all!

Ms. Metters: "Ha, that *would* be quite fun to organize. How did you get involved with such a specific organization?"

So she is down-to-earth. Interesting…

Cat: "Well, my best friend growing up, who is adopted from Korea, has a cleft palate. Until her adopted parents could afford the proper surgery, she had a difficult life. Watching her struggle was heartbreaking…so I slowly got involved in creating awareness and fundraisers for kids similar to Deena and their families."

Was that too personal? It was, and I shouldn't have used Deena by her first name. Stop fidgeting, Cat! No one wants to see you twirly-dirly your hair!

Wow! Well-rounded doesn't even begin to describe this girl. What's her name again? Cat King. I need to send her to the sales department and see what Dan thinks of her.

Ms. Metters: "Well, Cat, that is truly inspirational. Thank you so much for coming in today and telling me a bit more about yourself. It's always great matching a face to a resume. Just to let you know, I am not directly in charge of hiring, but I believe Dan, the head of our Sales Department, would be interested in talking with you further."

Cat: "Oh! That would be great!"

Yaaaay! Now what do I do?...Oh my gosh, I never prepared on how to leave an interview!!!!

"Should I wait for him to contact me or should I…walk to his…office?"

Ms. Metters: "No, he will be in touch with you. It should be within the next week or so. He will most likely contact you via e-mail, so just keep an eye on your inbox."

Cat: "OK. Thank you again for your time, Ms. Metters. I look forward to meeting your sales manager. Hopefully I'll be working here soon! Fingers crossed!"

Too cutesy? Maybe, but I don't care! I'm getting a second interview! OK, well, maybe getting a second interview, but still Yay!!

Ms. Metters: "Well, regardless, I hope you find what you are looking for."

I think she'd be a good fit here, but the crossed-fingers thing is a bit immature.

Cat and Ms. Metters exchange 'goodbyes'. Jocolyn escorts Cat to the door. Saying goodbye over her shoulder, Cat finally has time to process the interview.

After the Interview

I think it went well…but who knows? Wait, she hardly told me anything about the job…great! So assuming I get the second interview, I'll be going in there blind! Whoa, whoa, whoa! Cat, no freaking out allowed until you actually get the interview. It would be awesome, though. Man, I need to keep on top of my e-mails!

Yes, she was nervous, but that's to be expected. She doesn't have experience, but has spunk and initiative—I love her involvement with the cleft palate organization. She's a well-rounded girl, worth a second look. I'm rooting for her!

Would You Give Cat a Second Interview?

☐ Yes, Cat was spacey at times but she deserves a second interview. Hopefully she'll have her nerves under control by the time she meets Dan!

☐ No, Cat took the interview too personal too often. She also doesn't have any experience. I'm afraid she will just try to get some experience here and then move on to bigger and better things.

Would You Hire This Person?

☐ Yes…because ____

☐ No…because ____

What the Interviewer Decided:

After speaking to Jocolyn about Cat, Dan brought Cat in for a second interview for a possible sales position. In that interview, a more relaxed Cat demonstrated she was proactive, organized, comfortable speaking to different types of people, and showed initiative in her volunteer work and extracurricular activities. Dan hired her as an entry-level inside sales representative for the insurance company. Maybe the crossed-fingers helped!

Ignorance Is No Excuse!

So you thought homework was a thing of the past now that you're out of school? Not so fast!

Did this job candidate do his homework before the interview…or is he going in clueless?

Will the interviewer ask questions that will uncover this misstep?

Will he hire this person?

Would you?

Meet Brian O'Connor, human resources specialist for Richter Corporation, an international company specializing in building equipment that applies adhesives in manufacturing operations. He is seeking an engineer for an entry-level position in new product development.

Meet Kevin Rosen. Kevin is a very bright young man who has just graduated from Georgia Tech. His excellent grades reflect his intelligence and discipline as a student. Kevin has been successful in all his academic endeavors because he is very smart and organized. But Kevin has neglected to do something very important before his interview...

The Interview

Mr. O'Connor enters the Human Resources waiting room. "Kevin Rosen?"
Kevin jams his cell phone into his pocket and jumps up to meet the company recruiter.

Mr. O'Connor: "Welcome, Kevin! Just follow me to my office and take a seat."

Kevin: "Thank you, sir. Thank you for taking the time to meet with me."

Mr. O'Connor: "So, Kevin, I see you attended Georgia Tech but your family lives in Michigan. Why did you choose to go to college in another state?"

Kevin: "Well, I wanted to go to a top school. I wanted to challenge myself and get a degree from a top institution. I felt that would go a long way when I applied for a job. I remember my parents weren't too happy about the cost of out-of-state tuition, but I kept telling them it would be worth it."

Mr. O'Connor: "Well, I'm sure they are proud of you and feel they made a good investment in your future. Your grades are excellent. Did you find Georgia Tech challenging?"

Kevin: "Yes, sir, I did. I had never gotten a C in my life before Tech. And I came precariously close to a D in my thermodynamics class. It was brutal! They had warned us in Orientation that Tech separates the men from the boys, and that is really true."

OK, he's normal. Just needed to establish that.

Mr. O'Connor: "So, Kevin, tell me why you want to work for Richter Corporation. What is it about our business that interests you?"

'What is it about your business that interests me?' What do you mean? You are looking for mechanical engineers and I'm a mechanical engineer.

Kevin: "Uh, oh, well, I know you have mechanical engineering openings. I really like to work with things, figure out how they work and make them work better. It's like a personal challenge to me."

Mr. O'Connor: "What do you know about the company?"

I'll give him another chance to take the bait. Please don't tell me he doesn't know anything about our business. I don't expect him to know everything, but he at least needs to know that we make adhesive application systems!

This guy's making me nervous. I hope he doesn't see me sweating. How would I know about what they do? I know—I'll just tell him I'll work on any product they have.

Kevin: "Uh, I do know that Richter is very successful. I'm willing to work on any products you make at Richter Corporation. I'm willing to learn from the ground up. I have no problem working long hours or weekends or whatever you need."

Why is he harping on this? Let's move on to something else, please!

OK, that's enough. He evidently didn't do any research on the company.

Mr. O'Connor: "OK, Kevin, I see you had an internship with a company near Georgia Tech's campus. What did you do there?"

Kevin: "I shadowed another engineer and assisted him with programming, some spreadsheet designs, and some basic product design. It was an eye-opener for me because I just didn't know exactly what an engineer would do on a day-to-day basis."

Mr. O'Connor: "What most surprised you about the daily work of an engineer?"

Kevin: "Well, I learned that interpersonal communication is really important. A lot of engineers are the kinds of people who like to work alone, but they have to communicate with a lot of other departments every day to do their job. I'm more of an extrovert than the stereotypical engineer, so that was fine with me."

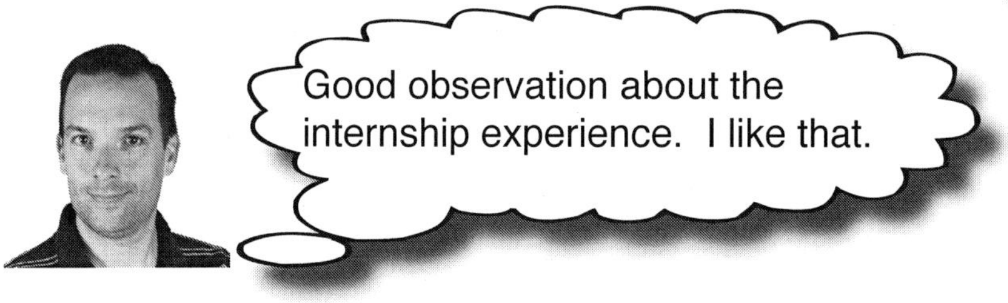

Mr. O'Connor: "Kevin, you have very good qualifications so I'm going to send your information to Lisa Phelps in our Consumer Products Division for consideration. If they want to interview you, I'll be in touch with you again by e-mail. Thank you for your time."

Kevin: "It was a pleasure meeting you. I hope Richter Corporation will give me an opportunity to show you what I can do. I'm a very hard worker!"

Brian gets up and shakes Kevin's hand before leading him back to the waiting room exit door. Kevin's mind races as he heads to his car.

After the Interview

So, maybe I'll hear from the Consumer Products Division! Hmmmm...I wonder what consumer products Richter is involved in making?

I have mixed feelings. He's articulate, smart, and has good grades from a very good school, but not knowing anything about the company concerns me. I'll have to think about recommending him for a second interview.

Would You Give Kevin a Second Interview?

☐ Yes, Kevin had very good grades, an engineering internship, and is willing to work in any position the company has available.

☐ No, Kevin broke one of the cardinal rules of an interviewee: not researching the employer ahead of time. A job seeker needs to do his or her homework to show they know about the company and want to be hired.

Would You Hire This Person?

☐ Yes...because ______________________________

☐ No...because ______________________________

What the Interviewer Decided:

Brian suggested that Kevin Rosen be brought back for a second interview, hoping that he would get the hint and research Richter Corporation and its customers. When Lisa Phelps asked similar questions, it was clear that Kevin had not gotten the message. Kevin, a very smart young man, had always relied on his IQ for his success. This time he needed common sense and good old-fashioned preparation.

Be a Positive, Not a Negative!

Everyone runs into a few "bad apples" in life—those people who, for whatever reason, try to make your life miserable. Can a few bad apples ruin a job interview?

Can this job candidate turn a negative into a positive, or is she stuck in the past?

Will the interviewer step on a "thorny" subject?

Will he hire this person?

Would you?

Meet Leon Felton, human resources manager for Chang & Wells, a growing Richmond, Virginia accounting firm. He is looking for an entry-level staff accountant to work with clients in Richmond and other cities in the southeastern U.S.

Meet Elizabeth Proust. Elizabeth has just received a B.B.A. degree from Virginia State College. Elizabeth is quick with numbers, logical, and organized. She worked part time for a Certified Public Accountant during tax season while she finished her last semester. Will that experience help her or hurt her during her interview? It's all about attitude!

The Interview

Elizabeth turns in her chair as she hears footsteps in the hall behind her. Mr. Felton holds out his hand to greet her with a handshake. Elizabeth stands quickly, dumping her purse on the floor. She scrambles to jam everything back into her bag.

Mr. Felton *(laughing and smiling)*: "Well, hello, Elizabeth! Can I help you pick up your things?"

Elizabeth: "Oh, no, sir! I'll be fine. I travel pretty light compared to most of my friends."

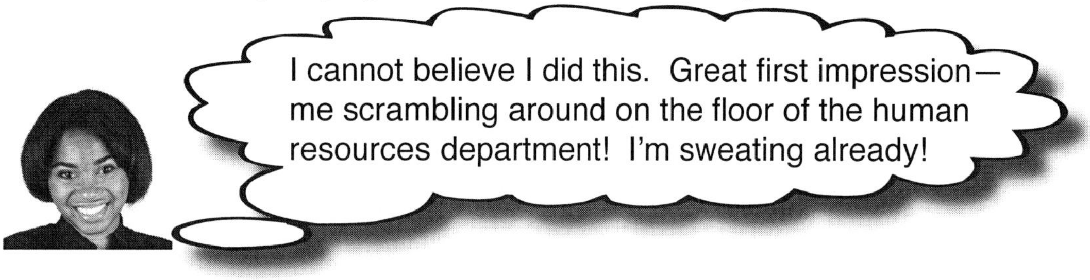

Mr. Felton: "Come on back to my office. Traveling light is a good thing in a job like this. We sometimes send accountants to work in our clients' offices out of town, so life is just easier if you don't have a lot of stuff to lug around."

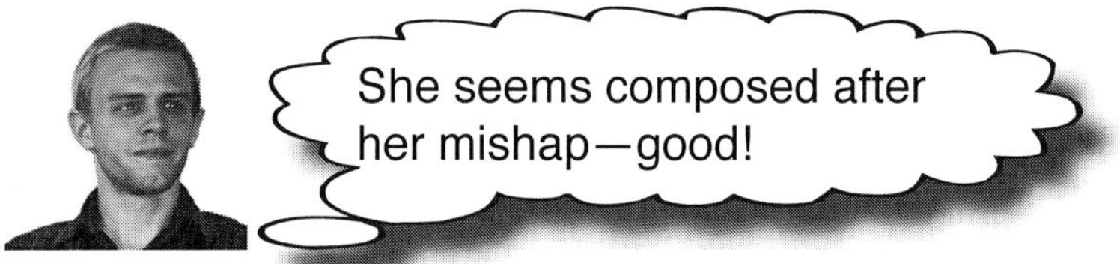

Elizabeth: "That sounds great. I like to be organized—a place for everything and everything in its place!"

Mr. Felton: "I'd say that's definitely a good trait for an accountant. So, tell me why did you choose accounting for your major?"

Elizabeth: "Well, I had a math teacher in high school who wanted students to understand the work world. He talked to us from time to time about careers that were math-related. He called accounting the "language of business" and said that today's accountants do much more than crunch numbers...and he said that an accounting background can launch you into a number of business careers. I've always been good in math, and I remembered what he said when it came time to choose a career."

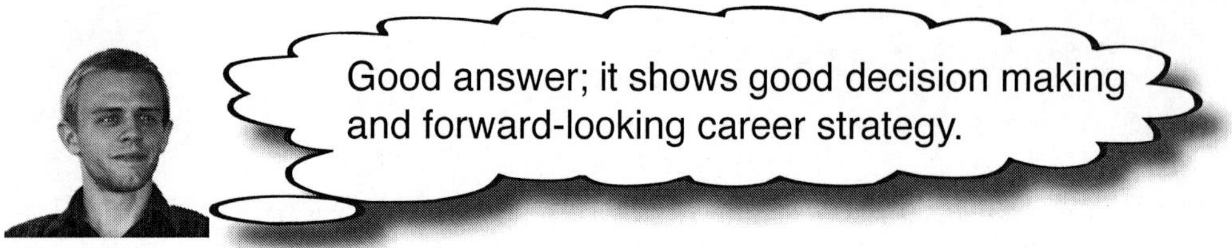

Mr. Felton: "I see you had an internship with a CPA. How did that go?"

Elizabeth: "I learned a lot and realized how important accounting is to the survival of a business, for sure. When I was there, most of the work revolved around individual tax returns, but Mr. Claiborne had some corporate returns underway at the same time. I worked some long hours during tax season! I got some great experience but it was hard to tell if he was pleased with anything because he was just really difficult to work with. He didn't like questions, but I had to ask them to understand what to do."

Mr. Felton: "So how did you deal with that difficult working environment?"

Elizabeth: "It bothered me because I am conscientious and always want to do a good job. It's not easy to work for someone you don't like personally. I had a professor in my last semester in college who was the same way. Nothing pleased him, and it was like pulling teeth to get answers to questions. I learned in that situation that you can only do your best—some people are not going to like you, but you just do your job and find a way to complete a task. I kept telling myself that while working for Mr. Claiborne."

Mr. Felton: "What are some strategies you used when you couldn't get the answers you needed from your professor or your supervisor?"

Elizabeth: "I researched things on my own. I also asked the one other accountant in the office to help me. He was young like me, but we put our heads together and figured out lots of things. That was a real feeling of accomplishment!"

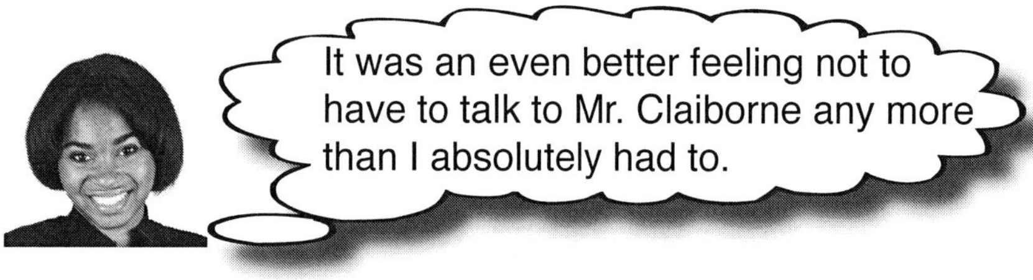

Mr. Felton: "How do you feel about your supervisor now? Did you leave on good terms?"

Elizabeth: "Yes, we left on good terms. I may not like him personally, but I never let him know that. I think he is just an unhappy person, and I could not help that. I did my job and I know I contributed greatly while I was there. He was able to take on more clients because of all the work I did behind the scenes."

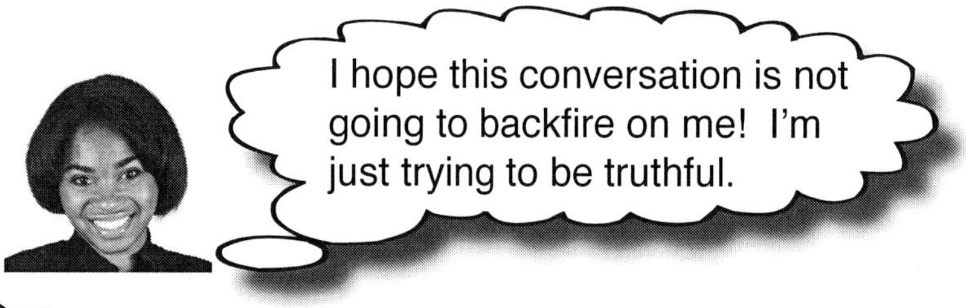

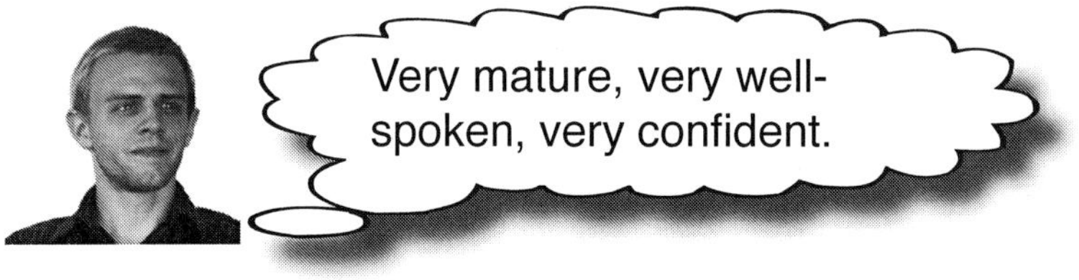

Mr. Felton: "Elizabeth, I'm very glad to have met you. I'm going to send your resume to Ronald Spain, our Accounting Supervisor. It may take him a few weeks to review all the candidates, but we'll be in touch by e-mail if you are selected for a second interview."

Elizabeth: "Thank you! I enjoyed meeting you as well. I hope I can come back for another interview to discuss the position more fully and expand on my qualifications. And next time, I'll make sure my purse zipper is closed so I don't drop my life on the floor!"

Mr. Felton laughes and escorts Elizabeth to the door. They shake hands again before exchanging goodbyes.

After the Interview

I think things went well, even though he really zoned in on how it was to work with Mr. Claiborne. Oh, well, that's water under the bridge, and I think it's always right to tell the truth about a situation.

Very impressed! She turned a negative situation into a positive one. The workplace is full of difficult people and personality conflicts, and she's learned some valuable lessons early. And I like her sense of humor!

Would You Give Elizabeth a Second Interview?

☐ Yes, Elizabeth has good experience, good grades, and a good attitude. She handled a negative situation well, and was able to explain that simply to the interviewer.

☐ No, Elizabeth made a mistake talking about her prior supervisor. She should not have even brought up the fact that he was difficult to work with.

Would You Hire This Person?

☐ Yes...because ____

☐ No...because ____

What the Interviewer Decided:

Mr. Felton highly recommended that Elizabeth be brought back for a second interview. Elizabeth impressed the Accounting Supervisor as well when she expanded on her work experience and extra-curricular activities as her sorority treasurer. He needed a mature candidate to work with out-of-state clients, and hired Elizabeth to fill the open accounting position. She used her first paycheck to buy a new purse.

Better Late Than Never...Or Not?

On-time arrival is crucial to success in business…and in life!

Will this job candidate make it to the interview on time?

If she doesn't, will the interviewer give her a chance, or show her the door?

Will he hire this person?

Would you?

Meet Evan Freeman, top chef for The Passion, one of the top restaurants in downtown Dallas. He is looking for a pastry chef trainee. He likes to train his own people so they become experts in designing and making The Passion's magnificent treats.

Meet Teresa Mason. Teresa is sensitive, creative, passionate about everything she does...but is chronically late. She knows it, and vows virtually every day to change her ways. She was determined to be on time to this interview this morning, but...

The Interview

Evan Freeman checks his watch. His interview candidate should have arrived twenty minutes ago. He glances out the window to see a young woman in a blue suit and black, four-inch heels scurrying up the sidewalk to the front door of The Passion. Evan opens the door to greet her.

Mr. Freeman: "Are you Teresa Mason, by any chance?"

Teresa *(breathless after racing from her car in high heels):* "Oh, yes, sir, I am."

Mr. Freeman: "I'm Evan Freeman, the Executive Sous Chef here at The Passion. Just follow me over to this table and let's sit down."

Teresa: "I'm so sorry I'm late. I was stuck in traffic. I guess I should have left earlier."

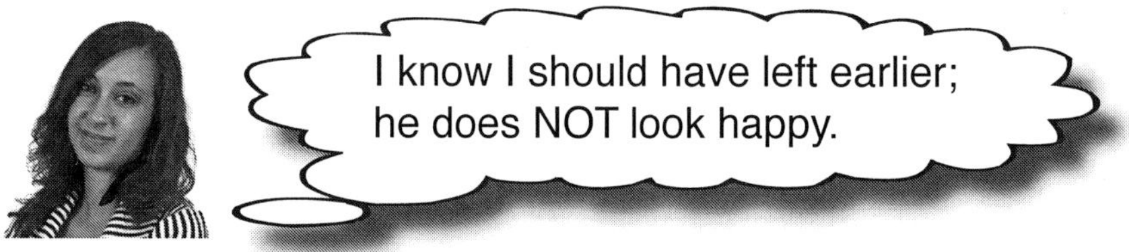

Mr. Freeman: "Well, I'm very busy today with interviews and only have a few minutes to spend with you. I understand you are interested in becoming a pastry chef with us. Besides your extensive experience in front of the house, what qualifies you to become a chef—specifically a pastry chef here at The Passion?"

Teresa: "Well, as you mentioned, I've worked in the restaurant industry since tenth grade. Although I've been serving and hostessing, that gave me a great deal of experience and introduced me to the idea of cooking professionally. So I went to a two-year culinary school and found that I loved doing more than just cooking—I wanted to create my own masterpieces! As far as becoming pastry chef, I've always enjoyed baking sweets and treats and I can really use my creative side in that area."

Mr. Freeman: "And you believe your baking hobby qualifies you to become a pastry chef at one of the most prestigious restaurants in Dallas?"

Teresa: "It is much more than a hobby, sir. I love to cook and create! No, I don't have any direct experience being a pastry chef, but since the time I could walk, I've been experimenting in my mom's kitchen with cakes, candy, and pies. I'm willing to learn your style from the ground up. And personally, I believe passion should trump experience any day."

Mr. Freeman *(smiling with mild amusement):* "Well, we do want our employees to be passionate about their jobs, but we also run a business. On your resume, I see a year-long gap when you were not working. What were you doing during that time period?"

Teresa: "My mother passed away during that time. I spent a lot of time at home helping my dad with arrangements and my younger siblings."

Mr. Freeman: "I'm very sorry to hear that, Teresa. That had to be a very difficult time."

Teresa: "Yes, sir, it was. Thank you."

Mr. Freeman: "Well, what is the flexibility of your schedule? In other words, when would you be able to work?"

Teresa: "My schedule right now is pretty tight. I'm still serving at Darla's Diner full-time, but in the event of getting this job, I could start once my two-week notice has expired."

Mr. Freeman: "What about weekends and nights? Are you willing to work those shifts as well?"

Teresa: "Yes, I know weekends are a must in the restaurant industry and I am OK with it as long as it's not every weekend."

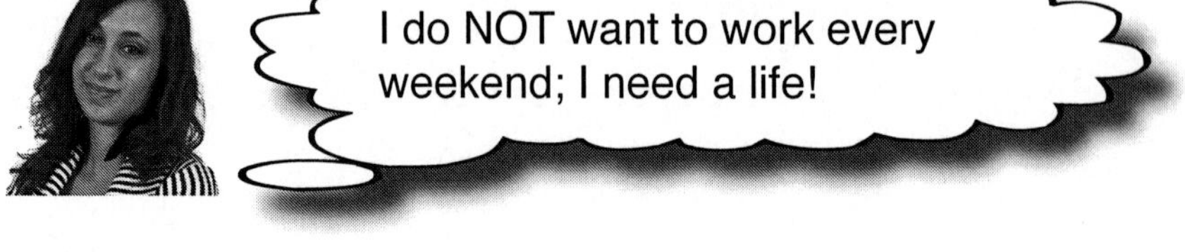

Hmmm...has a weekend issue, I see.

Mr. Freeman: "I understand no one wants to work every weekend, but a trainee might have to pay their dues for a while. *(He shuffles and stacks papers.)* Well, Teresa, you have given us a lot to consider. I wish we could talk longer, but as I said, I am very busy today with other interviews. If we are interested in a second interview, our executive chef will be speaking with you at that time. Do you have any questions for me?"

Teresa: "No sir, not at this time. And again, I'm so sorry for being late. That awful Dallas traffic really got me today."

Does that sound like an excuse?
Oh, man, am I blowing it?

Mr. Freeman: "I understand that we're all late sometimes. Thank you for your time, Teresa, and have a great day."

Teresa: "Thank you, you too. It was a pleasure meeting you!"

Teresa shakes Mr. Freeman's hand before click-clacking across the glossy tile floor in her heels. She shrugs her shoulders; she does not know what to think about her short interview.

After the Interview

I hope I come back for a second interview. Who knows... he was a bit testy. Yes, I was late, but I apologized! And the comment about paying my dues as a trainee—I guess this job means my weekends are done—for a long time. That stinks!

Teresa seems creative, passionate, and she wants to be in the restaurant business. But being late to the interview is a huge red flag to me. If she's late for something so important, will she be late to work every day?

Would You Give Teresa a Second Interview?

☐ Yes, she seems genuine and honest. She is creative, willing to learn, and she's passionate.

☐ Heck no! She was late. You CANNOT be late for interviews, period. Plus, she was unhappy about working weekends. Sorry, this is a seven-day-a-week business.

Would You Hire This Person?

☐ Yes…because ____

☐ No…because ____

What the Interviewer Decided:

Unfortunately, Teresa's late arrival and attitude about working weekends worked against her. Mr. Freeman contacted Teresa to say that he had chosen another candidate for the position. The pastry chef they hired had no culinary schooling, but had been a sous chef, butcher, and baker for a total of three years. His experience, on-time arrival to his interview, and positive attitude made him more appealing to the restaurant's management. A not so sweet ending for Teresa.

The ability to concentrate and use time well is everything.— Lee Iacocca

Show Me the Money-NOT!

Everyone wants to know what the salary will be when interviewing for a job.

This job candidate just can't wait to pop the question—"How much?"

Will the interviewer be turned off?

Will he hire this person?

Would you?

Meet Matt Staple, manager of Human Resources for Mirco, one of the top five video game developers in the United States. He is seeking an entry-level programmer for the company's rapidly expanding action/ adventure game division.

Meet Samantha Harris, or "Sam." Sam is a smart, creative, strong-willed young woman determined to work in the video game industry. Sam is a bit quirky, and tact and social graces often escape her. Will she offend the interviewer with some of her odd behavior?

The Interview

Matt Staple enters Mirco's crowded waiting room outside Human Resources. He notices one young woman completely engrossed in watching a Mirco video game demonstration on a massive wall television. The others in the waiting room are flipping through magazines.

Mr. Staple: "Samantha Harris?"

Heads swing around in the waiting room filled with video games to sample, but no one stands up. He tries again. "Samantha Harris?"

Sam *(jumping to her feet):* "Oh! I'm here!"

Mr. Staple: "Hi Samantha. I am Matt Staple, manager of Human Resources. How are you today? Come on in."

Sam: "Hello, Mr. Staple. Please just call me Sam. Too much tomboy in me for such a girly name, if you know what I mean."

Mr. Staple: "Well, Sam, welcome to Mirco. I see you are interested in becoming a programmer here. Why do you want to work here?"

Sam: "Yes, sir, I'm very interested in Mirco. Everything I've read tells me it's just an awesome, creative company. I've been following the company's growth for years, especially after the move from Chicago to San Jose. Things really took off after that, especially once Planet Smashers was released."

Mr. Staple: "I see you received your degree in interactive design and game development from the Savannah College of Art and Design, and that your grade point average is exceptional. What led you to choose this field?"

Sam: "Honestly, I'm a chick who has always loved video games. Heck, I still play my old Nintendo 64! Since I've loved gaming my whole life, I decided I should make a career of it. I mean, who doesn't want to get paid to learn, play, and design video games?!"

Mr. Staple: "And how do you stay current on trends and new software/technology now that you are out of school?"

Sam: "Since games are my passion, I naturally stay up to date just because I love them and play everything I can get my hands on. I am constantly reading about the newest technology and games. I like to find out what players say about games too. And I dabble with design all the time, just because it's fun."

Mr. Staple: "Working collaboratively is very important here at Mirco. How comfortable are you with working with others on a team effort?"

Sam: "Oh, I like to work together with others. Teamwork is great. When I get road-blocked, I can nudge my partner and get the fire burning again, you know?"

Mr. Staple: "What will you bring to the team?"

Sam: "Well, Mr. Staples, *(She pauses to collect her thoughts.)* I feel I can bring several things. One is passion for gaming. I just don't think you can make great games without a passion for them, you know? And I know I don't have a lot of experience, but I am a good programmer and am very detailed. I get lost in my work, and I want to make it right."

Mr. Staple: "So, how do you feel about crunching?"

Sam: "Oh, I've heard about crunch time and how crazy it can get before a deadline. I mean, I'm single, and I'd probably be home playing video games if I wasn't working overtime, so I'm OK with it."

Mr. Staple: "Well, Miss Harris, I'm glad you could make it in today for this preliminary interview. Do you have any questions for me?"

Sam: "Well, I was wondering what the pay range is for a programmer here."

I need to know to compare it to Zelasco's job offer!

Mr. Staple: "Well, Sam, we don't talk about compensation until a job offer is made. I hope you can understand that."

She should have learned not to ask that in Interview 101 class! Good grief.

Oh no, he thinks I'm an idiot. I've blown it.

Sam: "Oh, yes, sir, I understand. And I'm sorry for bringing it up. Thank you for taking the time to visit with me. It would be so amazing to work here. I've been dreaming of working for Mirco since I started college. So I really do appreciate this opportunity."

Mr. Staple: "It was a pleasure for me as well. Keep an eye on your e-mail. You will receive word from us by the end of the month if we'd like to bring you back for a more detailed interview."

Sam: "OK! Thank you, Mr. Staples. Bye!"

After the Interview

I hope, I hope, I hope they call me back. It would be so COOL to work for Mirco. Maybe I'll get an interview with a programmer and get to see where the action is. It's got to be awesome!

From her grades, it looks like she's a very smart girl. She handled herself well in the interview until she asked about the salary. I'm surprised she did that, but she got the message that it was not the time for that. I liked her. She wants to work here, I can tell that.

Would You Give Sam a Second Interview?

☐ Yes, Sam is smart, and she's very passionate about gaming. You can teach people a lot of things, but you can't teach them passion.

☐ No, Sam was kind of ditzy in the waiting room and asked about compensation way too early in the process. Those are game-changers.

Would You Hire This Person?

☐ Yes...because ______________________________

☐ No...because ______________________________

What the Interviewer Decided:

Sam returned for a second interview with Mirco's head of programming. They clicked immediately—you could say they were kindred spirits when it came to video gaming! Sam was hired soon after as an entry-level programmer. She's working on a new action/adventure game set in Antarctica called "Frozen Frontier." And she's loving it—Sam even wears a big, fluffy parka to work every day to get in the mood! Sam is so cool!!

The successful person makes a habit of doing what the failing person doesn't like to do.— Thomas Edison

Will a Lack of Schooling Hurt Him?

Education is the stepping stone to opportunity.

Can experience overcome a lack of formal education?

Will this candidate's experience get him the job?

What do you think?

Would you hire this person?

Meet Clayton Childs, Human Resources Director at LaFly Airlines. Due to new international routes, LaFly is looking for mechanics, pilots, and other support personnel. Today, he is specifically interviewing for aircraft mechanic positions. He is looking for qualified candidates who are self-motivated "do-ers"!

Meet Mike Harvey, a country boy able to fix just about anything! He made average grades in high school, partially due to ADD undiagnosed until his senior year. But Mike has found his true passion: airplanes! He worked his way up from loading bags to maintenance man at Delinear Air. Now he is hoping to land an aircraft mechanic position with LaFly Airlines.

The Interview

Mr. Childs: "Hey, Mike, come on in. Take a seat."

Mike: "Thank you, sir."

Mr. Childs: "Sir? *(laughs)* Do I really look that old? You can call me Clayton. Well, let's jump right into it. As you know from our website, we just opened a new international section to our airport and are looking for qualified aircraft mechanics. I see here on your resume that you have experience, but could you please tell me a little more about the jobs you've had?"

Mike: "Well, Mr. Childs….I mean…Clayton, when I finished high school, I began working at Delinear Air loading luggage onto planes. I worked my way into the maintenance shop. That's where I got my required hours of experience working on airframes and powerplants. And just this last month, I passed my tests and I'm waiting on my Airframe and Powerplant licenses now."

Mr. Childs: "Impressive. I see you were promoted within the first three months at Delinear."

Mike: "Yes. I was just so fascinated with the inner workings of such crazy big planes. I loved being there so I learned all I could, stayed late and came in early. Plus, I am a little ADD, so the maintenance shop was ideal, with jobs changing daily."

Mr. Childs: "And what makes you believe you are an ideal candidate to work here at LaFly?"

Mike: "Besides my winning personality? *(laughs)* But seriously, I think LaFly is perfect for me. I am experienced, a hard worker, and extremely cautious, double-checking my work multiple times to ensure the integrity of the plane. I love solving problems and fixing things too. While other kids wanted an Xbox, I wanted anything mechanical to tinker with and fix."

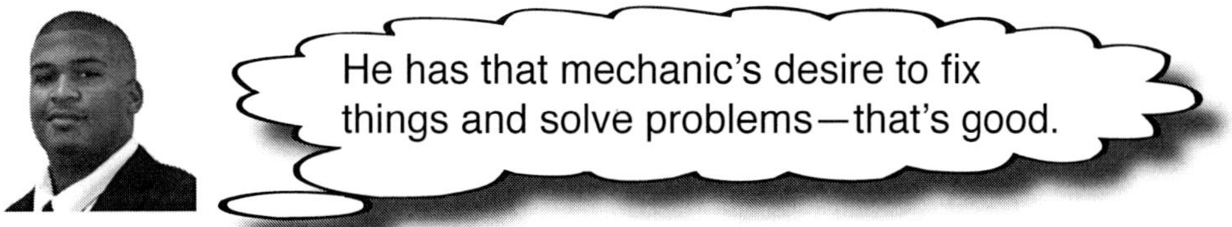

Mr. Childs: "And what is your preferred plane to work on?"

Mike: "That's tough…I'd probably have to say the Boeing 737. It's the workhorse of just about every airline fleet. I read the other day that it's the world's best-selling aircraft, and it's really reliable. I've been working on it the longest and I feel very comfortable around it."

Mr. Childs: "So are you uncomfortable working on other planes then?"

Mike: "Oh no, sir, not at all. You asked what my favorite was and it's the Boeing 737."

Mr. Childs: "You're right; I did ask...I'm glad to know you are flexible to work on all body types. And how long do you think you would stay with us here at LaFly?"

Mike: "I'm a loyal worker and would not expect to leave unless there was no opportunity for advancement. So you may be stuck with me permanently!"

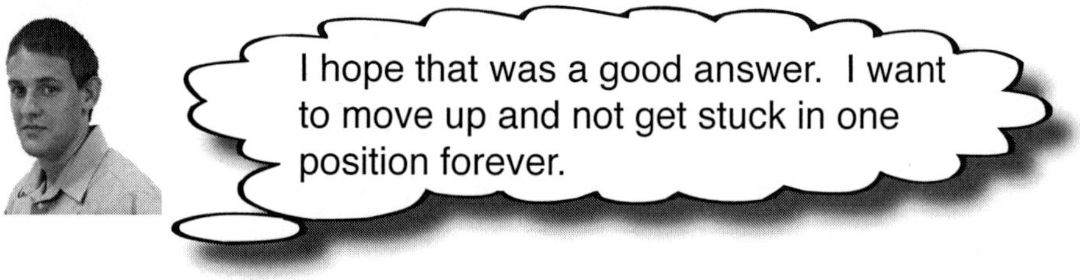

Mr. Childs: "We'll see how the interview goes first. You mentioned before that you have ADD issues. Do you think that will hinder your work performance here?"

Mike *(laughing)*: "If anything, it helps! Working on these planes, going from hangar to hangar, solving new problem after new problem, makes me feel like I don't have ADD, but that my job does and I love it. Controlling chaos is the name of the game, right?"

Mr. Childs *(smiling)*: "Well, too much chaos is not a good thing, right? OK, speaking of chaos, can you recall a time when you were faced with a pressure-packed situation, and tell me how you handled it?"

Mike *(pausing)*: "Well, uh, when you have a maintenance problem, you feel pressure to fix things so the flight can continue on schedule. But our company philosophy is to fix things right, no matter what it takes. I can't remember a specific instance, but when I have a checklist to follow, I follow it. I don't care who is breathing down my neck, I follow the rules and never skip a step. You just can't cut corners with airplanes, you know? I learned that very early in this job. People's lives are on the line!"

Mr. Childs: "You are right about that, Mike, and I'm glad to hear you are so conscientious. That's an essential character trait to have in this business. Well, it has been a pleasure meeting you. I'll be looking into your references and be back in touch with you soon. Is there anything you'd like to ask before we finish?"

Mike: "Yes, when can I start? *(They both laugh.)* Seriously though, what are my chances with LaFly? I'm worried that since I haven't been able to afford a tech school or college, I will be passed over."

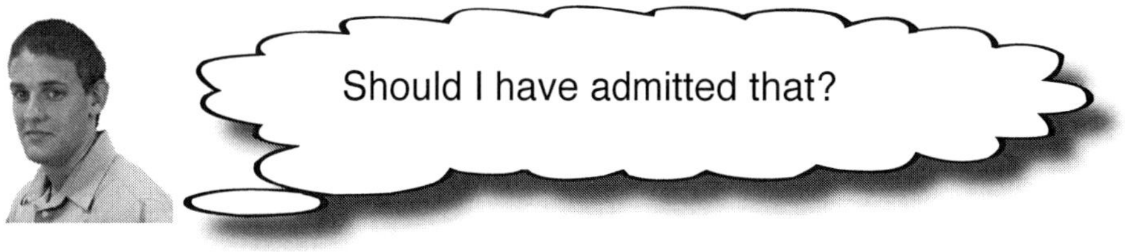

Mr. Childs: "I'm not going to lie, schooling is an attractive quality in a candidate, but your experience is also invaluable. I guess what I'm trying to say is don't worry. Experience is just as valuable here as education. Sometimes moreso."

Mike: "I'm glad to hear that. And on that note, I'll let you get back to your day. Thank you again for the opportunity to come in and interview. I really hope I get the job."

Mr. Childs: "Really great talking with you. I will be in touch if we'd like to bring you back for a second interview. Have a great day."

After the Interview

He's a very down-to-earth guy and looks to be qualified. Had a great, strong handshake, too. I like that. He needs to hurry up and get those licenses, though. They must be on file before being hired. I'd like to have the maintenance supervisor talk to him and see what he thinks.

Would You Give Mike a Second Interview?

☐ Yes, Mike is personable with experience, drive, and a love of airplanes. I definitely recommend him for a follow-up interview.

☐ No, Mike has experience, but in this job market we require both experience and education.

Would You Hire This Person?

☐ Yes...because ______________________________

☐ No...because ______________________________

What the Interviewer Decided:

Ten days after Mike's interview, Mr. Childs called and invited Mike for a second interview with an aircraft maintenance supervisor. After the interview, LaFly hired Mike for a 90-day probation period. After 90 days, Mike will either be offered a full-time position with LaFly or he will be respectfully asked to leave. Keep your fingers crossed for Mike! A probation period is his chance to shine.

Too many people overvalue what they are not and undervalue what they are.— Malcolm Forbes

What Does Your Body Language Say About You?

Our body language speaks volumes about us.

Will this job candidate's body language hurt his chances of getting the job?

Will the interviewer give him the hint to literally "straighten up"?

Will he hire this person?

Would you?

Meet Kurt Wells, vice principal at Gordon Heights Middle School. He's a seasoned veteran of middle school hallways and is looking for a new 7th grade counselor. A qualified candidate needs to have the proper education, but Mr. Wells is really looking for a counselor who can empathize with students in the rough middle school years.

Meet Andy Preacher. After teaching art for several years, he wants to try his hand at guidance counseling. He's a laid-back kind of guy, and feels confident that his experience and academic accomplishments will impress his potential employer. He also truly wants to help kids, and feels that will come through loud and clear. Little does he know something else will ring a bit louder...

The Interview

Mr. Wells: "Hey Andy, how are you today? Come on in."

His hair is kind of long for my liking, but middle school kids will like think he's cool.

Andy slumps to the side of his chair as he settles in for the interview.

Andy: "Hello, Mr. Wells. Glad to meet you. I'm doing well…I'm here, so I have no complaints."

OK…that's a bit of a negative comment to start.

Mr. Wells: "Well, that's the first step. So, you are interested in becoming our 7th grade guidance counselor. Why the change from art teacher to guidance counselor?"

Andy: "I'm glad you asked. I love teaching art—one reason is because it's so therapeutic. It's an expression of emotion and individuality. While teaching, I learned that I could help students embrace and express their feelings in a healthy, safe environment. I wanted to advance my career, and continue to help kids, so I decided to move into the counseling arena. Needless to say, I went back to school and got my Master's in Education in School Counseling."

Mr. Wells: "And do you have any other training in counseling?"

Andy: "Besides the 100-hour required practicum, I've completed more than 200 hours of internships through private and public counseling offices."

Mr. Wells: "That's quite a bit of time. You say 'private offices.' What exactly does that entail?"

I really wish he'd sit up straight in his chair. This is annoying me.

Andy: "I worked in a counselor's office that specialized in working with troubled teens. These were teens with addiction issues, unstable family lives, and teens who were just confused and felt alone with no one to talk to."

Mr. Wells: "Does it not interest you more to stay within the private sector?"

Andy: "You know, the private sector doesn't appeal to me. Between insurance aggravation and parents forcing their kids to come in, I just don't like it. I feel I can help more people in the public school system. And honestly, I'd prefer helping more people to owning my own business."

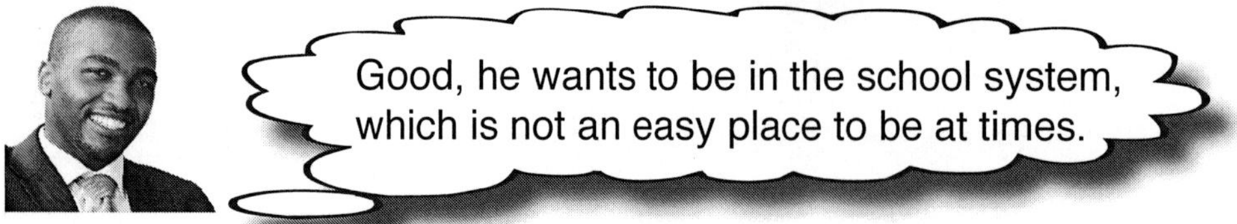

Mr. Wells: "And is there any one teenager or child who has truly made an impact on you?"

Andy: "Actually, all of them have. Every child has a unique story."

Mr. Wells: "Interesting…and why do you feel middle school guidance counseling is the perfect fit for you?"

Andy: "I believe middle school is one of the hardest transition periods in a kid's life. And today, with technology and media bombarding the youth and both parents working, I feel that's where I'm needed the most. *(Andy leans forward in his chair, out of his slump.)* Another thing I bring to the table is that I often suggest art therapy for kids. It can help them work out some of the things that are bothering them."

Mr. Wells: "That's really interesting, and you're right about middle school being very hard for a lot of students. *(He shuffles papers and looks at Andy over his glasses.)* Do you have any questions for me? Wait…do you hear that?"

(Andy's musical cell phone ringtone gets louder and louder as he fumbles in his pocket to turn it off.)

Andy *(red-faced with embarrassment)*: "I am so, so sorry. My kid brother must have changed my ringtone again."

"The Thong Song"—are you serious???

Mr. Wells: "These things happen, Andy. Yours isn't the first cell phone to ring in my office, and it won't be the last, I'm sure. Thank you for coming in today. I'll be in touch if we'd like you to come back for a second interview."

Mr. Wells opens the door. Andy, frazzled, trips over the chair leg as he tries to leave.

Andy: "Again, I'm sorry about that interruption. And, uhh, I will be in touch if I don't hear from you by the end of the week, if that is OK."

This is going from bad to worse—the phone, and now I trip!

Mr. Wells: "That's fine. E-mail is the best way to communicate, so here's my card with my e-mail address on it. Have a great day, Andy."

After the Interview

He is qualified and experienced. Seems smart and sensitive, and really cares for kids. But that slouch and that ringtone are not leaving me with a good feeling. Not much time to think about this now—I have lots of candidates to interview today.

I thought things were going well until my cell phone went off! I CANNOT believe I forgot to turn it off! What an idiot! And wait until I get a hold of Ryan. He needs to keep his hands off my phone. I hope they give me another chance; this is a good school!

Would You Give Andy a Second Interview?

☐ Yes, Andy is clearly qualified, and appears genuine about helping teens—ultimately that is the most important qualification. He made a mistake in forgetting to turn off the phone—we all forget things from time to time.

☐ No, You can't be a guidance counselor to middle schoolers—especially girls—with such a provocative ringtone. He says his brother put it on there, but could it have been Andy's choice? Most importantly, though, his body language during the interview was disrespectful and made him appear somewhat disinterested.

Would You Hire This Person?

☐ Yes…because ____

☐ No…because ____

What the Interviewer Decided:

A week after the interview, Mr. Wells called Andy and asked him to come in for a second interview. The school principal wanted to interview him. Although his cell phone was turned off this time, Andy's body language had not changed. He still appeared disengaged in the interview. Although Andy has great experience and a love for helping kids, he was not hired for the job.

It is our choices…that show what we truly are, far more than our abilities.— J.K. Rowling

Think Before You Speak!

It's always a good idea to think before you speak.

This job candidate pauses to gather his thoughts more than once. Is that a little too often?

Will this give the interviewer the wrong impression?

Will he hire this person?

Would you?

Meet Amir Karam, personnel director of High Tech Press. He is looking for a smart, savvy writer to tackle some complex, technical projects. The job is high-pressure with tight deadlines. The person he hires needs to be smart, confident, and capable.

Meet Henry Li. Henry loves to write! As a child, he wrote stories just for fun and read them to his younger brother and sister. He's a good student and a quick learner, but really doesn't like school that much. He wants to launch his writing career, especially one where he can travel!

The Interview

KNOCK! KNOCK! Amir Karam's assistant, Pam, taps on the door of his impeccably neat corner office. "Mr. Li is here for his interview, Mr. Karam."

Mr. Karam *(whirling around in his chair)* "Have a seat, Henry. Welcome to HTP! We have tight deadlines today, so our interview might be short. Go ahead and tell me what you think you can do for us."

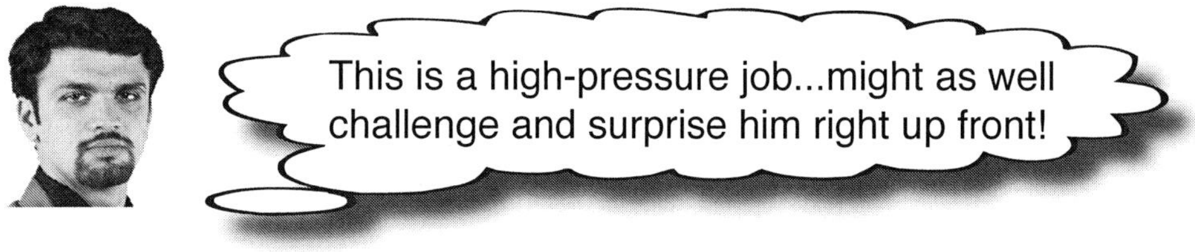

SILENCE SILENCE SILENCE

Henry *(with a deep confident sigh, then a smile)*: "Yes, Mr. Karam, I'd be glad to do that. I believe I've spent my entire life—so far, that is—preparing for this very position. I've been writing since I was very young, taken writing classes, and I enjoy learning and writing about the technical subjects that your company specializes in."

Mr. Karam: "Impressive, please go on."

SILENCE SILENCE SILENCE

Henry: "I started winning writing awards in fourth grade, you know, class essays, school-wide essays, even city and county writing contests. This success gave me confidence and let me learn to use my own voice and write with passion, from my heart and my head. It took some courage, but I like a challenge, and I liked informing people and seeing that light bulb go off in their heads."

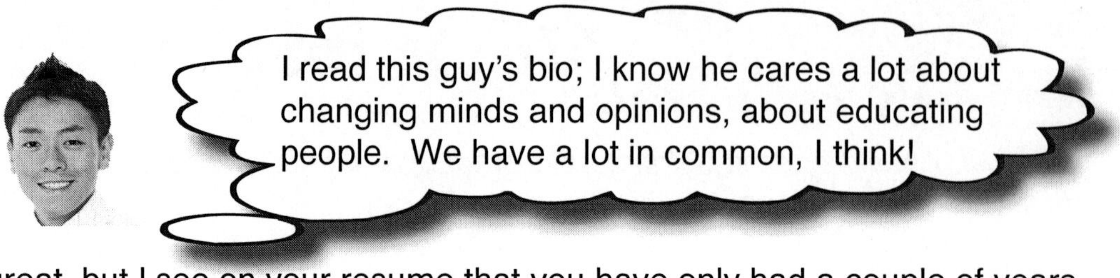

Mr. Karam: "That sounds great, but I see on your resume that you have only had a couple of years of community college. Why did you not go on to journalism school?"

Henry: "That's a very good question, sir. It seemed logical to take that approach and that's what my school counselor, senior English teacher, and, naturally, my parents recommended."

Henry flashes another one of those cryptic, whimsical smiles.

Mr. Karam: "So you're just naturally rebellious?"

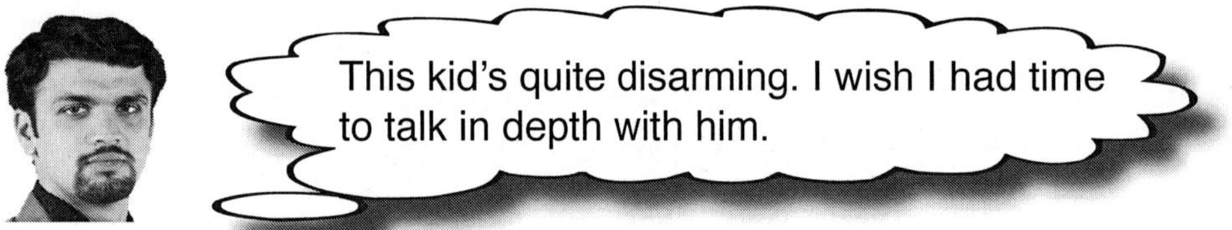

SILENCE SILENCE SILENCE…then a smile and shoulder shrug.

Henry: "Yes, sir, I certainly am. I felt that I could either continue to learn to write, or capitalize on the success I had during high school writing for a politician who was running for local office, writing speeches for my father who is the CEO of a large tech company, and creating marketing materials for some local businesses in major growth mode."

Mr. Karam: "So you just didn't think you had anything else to learn about writing?"

Henry: "Oh, no sir, absolutely not. I just thought that I could really focus on writing classes AND technical classes at community college so that I could specialize in technical topics and take those skills to get right to work. After all, some of my writing assignments took me out of state and even out of the country sometimes. My community college was very accommodating, and that was a big help."

Mr. Karam: "To be treated like a working adult, you mean?"

Henry: "Exactly."

Mr. Karam: "Well, we have work all around the world, Henry. What if your first assignment, right away, was in India? What would you say?"

SILENCE SILENCE SILENCE…then a slow smile.

Henry: "My bags can be ready to go in no time. Have laptop and cell phone, will travel."

Mr. Karam: "You certainly remind me of someone, Henry."

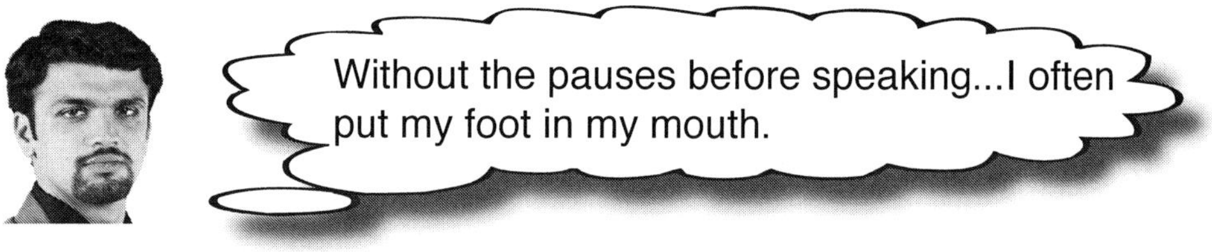

Henry *(laughing)*: "Hemingway? Kerouac? Cronkite? Yoda?"

Mr. Karam: "No, me…when I was your age."

Henry: "Well, sir, I take that as a compliment! I'm ready for any adventure High Tech Press might send my way. It's a big world out there and I'd love to see more of it and write about it."

Mr. Karam *(rising from his chair and reaching out to shake Henry's hand)*: "Well, Henry, it's been a pleasure to meet you. As you know, this was just a screening interview. I'll speak to our editors about bringing you back for a second interview. My assistant will be in touch."

Henry *(a slow smile spreading over his face)*: "Thank you so much, Mr. Karam. I'm so glad to have met you."

Pam escorts Henry back to the waiting room and says goodbye. Henry darts out into the rain toward his car.

After the Interview

I think I hit it off pretty well with Mr. Karam. He got my sense of humor, which plenty of people don't. And international travel as a writer—this could be my dream job!

Interesting young man—well-traveled, composed, thoughtful. We'll see what the editorial staff thinks when I forward his writing samples to them. That's where the rubber meets the road.

Would You Give Henry a Second Interview?

☐ Yes, Henry is a confident writer who is passionate about his craft. He loves to travel and work on technical subjects—a good fit for High Tech Press. His experience and writing samples trump a college degree with no experience.

☐ No, Henry should have a bachelor's degree. It's a very competitive job market out there, and a degree separates the men from the boys. Henry also hesitated before he answered several questions. That made me wonder if he was trying to say what he thought I wanted to hear instead of his true thoughts.

☐ Maybe—HTP could send him on a freelance assignment and see how he does.

Would You Hire This Person?

☐ Yes…because ____

☐ No…because ____

What the Interviewer Decided:

After checking Henry's references and reviewing his resume again, Mr. Karam could see Henry had been exceedingly modest about his talents and accomplishments. Mr. Karam urged the editorial staff to bring Henry in for a second inteview. After meeting Henry, the editors felt pretty sure they wanted to hire him, but decided to give Henry a freelance assignment first. Wish Henry luck—he's going to Gurgaon, India!

Control Your Inner "Control Freak!"

Our personalities signal who we are.

Will this job candidate be able to rein in her controlling nature…or will it slip out in the interview?

Will the interviewer be able to uncover the real girl under the interview façade?

What do you think?

Would you hire this person?

Meet Bob Holley, owner of Organize Your Life, a full-service organizing company that helps clients organize every facet of their lives, from a tiny linen closet to a massive company warehouse. He is seeking to hire two new organizers—people who can work easily with clients who are feeling overwhelmed about all their stuff!

Meet Maria Juarez. She organizes everything; she just can't help herself. When she goes to a friend's house, she secretly reorganizes the refrigerator contents when asked to grab the butter. When she visits her mom, she starts date-sorting the receipts on the counter. You get the picture...

The Interview

Maria Juarez arrives at Organize Your Life fifteen minutes early. As she waits in the reception area, she eyes the jumble of magazines on the coffee table. She has just finished straightening and alphabetizing them when Bob Holley greets her in the doorway.

Mr. Holley: "Good afternoon, Maria. Sorry if I've kept you waiting. Our weekly meeting went a little longer than expected today. Just follow me into my office right around the corner."

Maria: "That is not a problem, Mr. Holley. I'm just glad to be here."

Mr. Holley: "Well then, let's jump right in. I see you have been a file clerk for two years, and before that you were an administrative assistant. So how on earth did you decide to become a professional organizer and designer?"

Maria: "Well, I liked things to be neat growing up. I always color-coded my clothes. My toys were binned according to type of toy, and I've always been able to see my bedroom floor, unlike my brother's! *(They both laugh.)* But it was my last job that really opened my eyes to becoming a professional organizer."

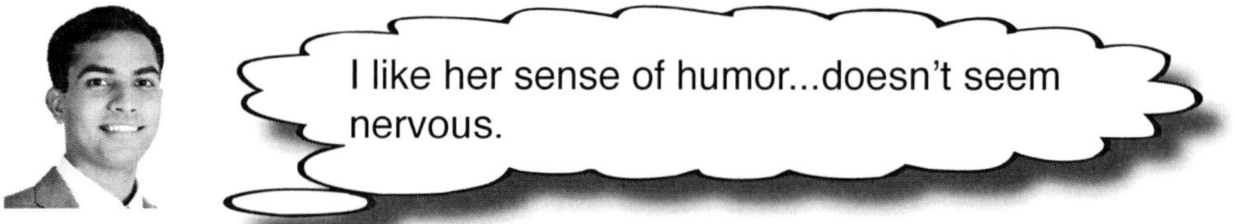

Mr. Holley: "How so?"

Maria: "Well, I noticed that while I was filing papers I naturally began reorganizing files, coding, and pretty much improving everything I could get my hands on. I even organized the janitor's closet!"

Mr. Holley: "Wow! So you are a bit of an organizer bug! I'm sure your co-workers appreciated your help."

Maria: "Actually, they were resistant at first, but eventually fell in love with my system."

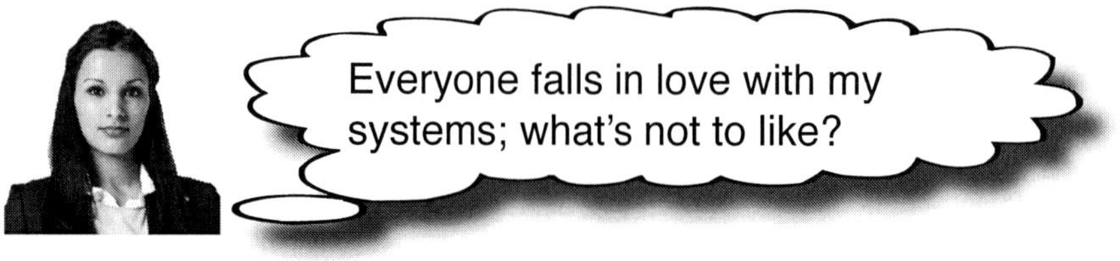

Mr. Holley: "So have you organized professionally or have you only done it to better streamline processes in your own life?"

Maria: "After finding my knack for organization, I started doing small projects for friends and people they referred me to for a reasonable fee."

Mr. Holley: "I'm sure that was appreciated as well. I see here that you prefer us not to contact your first employer, Mrs. Trammel. Is there any specific reason why?"

Maria: "Well, while working at Slate Industries, my boss, Mrs. Trammel, went on vacation for a week. While she was gone, I may have overstepped my boundaries a bit by cleaning and organizing her desk. She was not very happy when she got back to work and fired me on the spot. One thing I learned is don't mess with other people's stuff, no matter how much it needs organizing, without permission."

Mr. Holley: "That is unfortunate, but at least you learned a valuable lesson. Now, what is it that you expect from us here at Organize Your Life?"

Maria: "What do I expect from you?

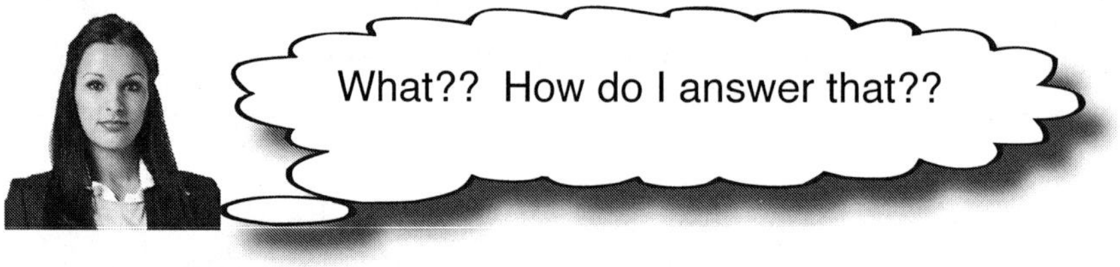

I'm not sure how to answer your question, but what I expect is to do what I love. Help people organize their lives, let go of unnecessary things, and better store things worth keeping."

Mr. Holley: "Do you have any experience with computer systems in your quest to unclutter the world?" *(chuckling lightly)*

Maria: "Yes, sir. I've familiarized myself with industry software and have invested in a new laptop. It has helped me tremendously with ideas and organization strategies."

Mr. Holley: "You 'familiarized' yourself?"

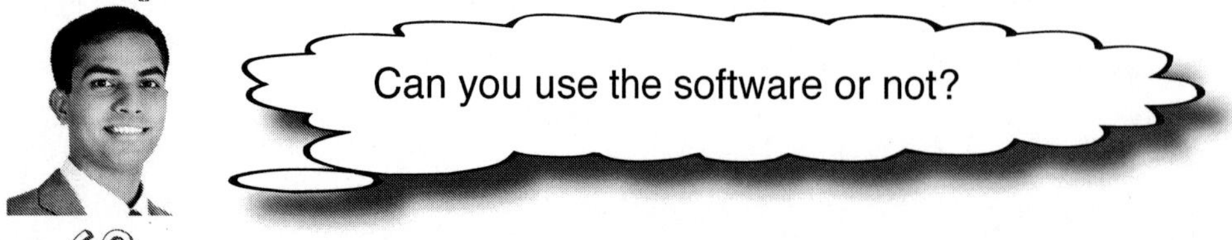

Maria: "Yes, I didn't know I would eventually be a professional organizer, so when I was still in high school, I didn't take computer classes. That's one of my regrets in life. So I taught myself, and it's worked out fine. I have a knack for computers."

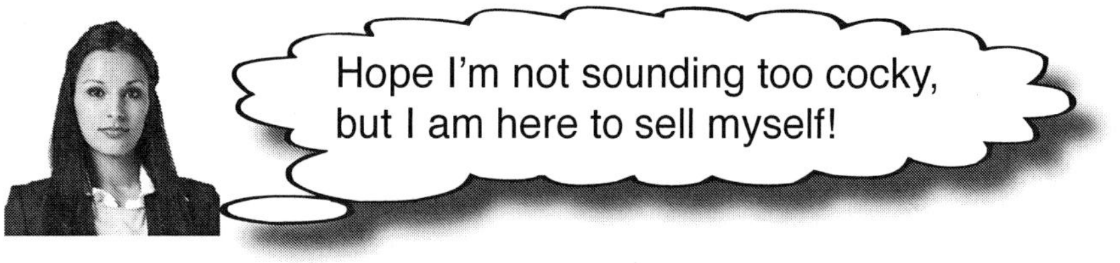

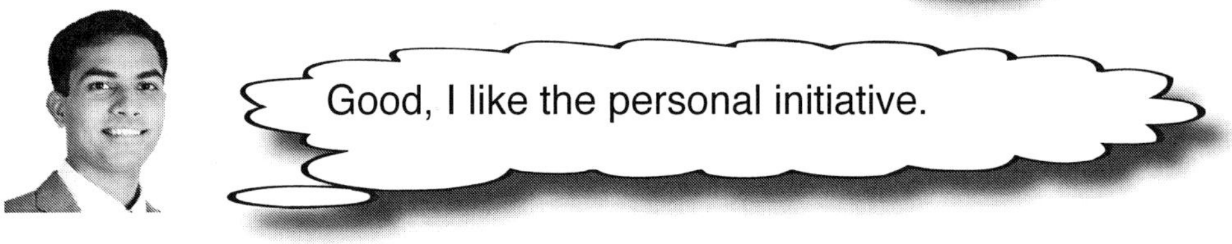

Mr. Holley: "And if I were to ask you to organize my desk right now, what would you do?"

Maria: "Thank goodness you asked! It's been driving me insane! You need to move your phone to the right of you, since I noticed you are right-handed. You also need a three-tiered inbox on your left corner to better utilize your desktop space: an inbox, outbox, and priority box. Then you need a large desk calendar to better organize your week without sticky-notes. And that chair—it's really out of style."

Mr. Holley: "Sounds like you have been dying to shout that out."

Maria: "I meant no offense by it…I'm just passionate I guess."

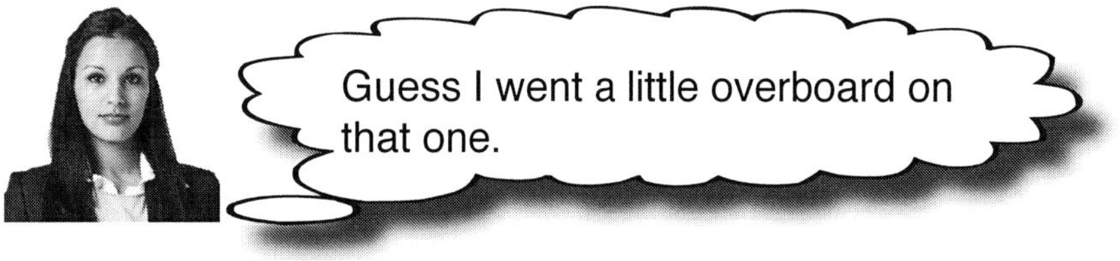

Mr. Holley *(chuckling)*: "That you are! Thank you for coming in today. This is just a short screening interview, but if you are considered for a second interview, we will be in touch by the end of the day. Please check your e-mail."

Maria: "Wow! That's so quick! Thank you, Mr. Holley. I hope you'll consider me for the organizer position. I would love to work for your company."

Maria heads out through the reception area. Mr. Holley stops to watch her as she heads toward the coffee table.

After the Interview

That place definitely needs work! Did you see that desk? I can whip them into shape in no time. Oh, good grief, someone has messed up the magazines again. Do I have to fix everything?

There she goes, stacking and sorting the magazines. I think she's smart, and a good organizer, but is she a little obsessive, and maybe too abrasive for our clients?

Would You Give Maria a Second Interview?

❒ Yes, Maria is a natural! Her knack for organizing and personal initiative will be real assets to Organize Your Life. It's not easy to find people with that natural ability.

❒ No, Maria appears to be controlling and unable to communicate appropriately with clients. A company's reputation in this business is everything, and one over-the-top employee can do tremendous damage.

Would You Hire This Person?

❒ Yes...because ____

❒ No...because ____

What the Interviewer Decided:

At the end of the business day, Mr. Holley called Maria and asked her to come in for a follow-up interview. During that interview, she vocalized her deep distaste for the decorating of the conference room and criticized the gallery of pictures outside the CEO's office. Maria was not hired. Instead, Maria works for herself. She does freelance organizing for churches, schools, and offices.

Can You Learn from Your Mistakes?

We all make mistakes in life. It's part of growing up.

Has this job candidate been able to learn from his mistakes while working in the family business?

Will the interviewer be pleased with his attitude…or alarmed by his past?

Would you hire this person?

Meet Lynne Kilgore, recruiter for Jonathan Entertainment Group (JEG), one of the country's top hotel chains. She is looking for a water slide tester. This little-known job will involve a lot of travel and requires a self-motivated person who can work independently, make repairs and recommendations, and report back to JEG management.

Meet Brian Kadel. Brian has experience in this field and hopes to better his salary and opportunities. He is single, loves to travel, and enjoys being outdoors. He knows how fortunate he is to be in a business where he can have fun and earn money at the same time!

The Interview

Ms. Kilgore scans the reception room where six to seven people are waiting.

Ms. Kilgore: "Mr. Kadel? Mr. Kadel? Mr. Kadel, are you here?"

Brian *(pulling out his earbuds when he sees Ms. Kilgore's eyes searching the room)*: "I'm so sorry! I wasn't expecting to be called back for a while. Are you ready for me?"

Ms. Kilgore: "Yes, Mr. Kadel. I am. I apologize for keeping you waiting. It's been a crazy morning. Please come in and take a seat."

Brian: "Oh, no need to apologize. I'm thankful to be here for an interview."

Ms. Kilgore: "Great! Well, Brian, we invited you in today because Jonathan Entertainment Group is looking for water slide testers since our hotel chain is expanding so rapidly. Now I see here that you have been testing water slides for the past four years. Can you tell me how you came into this career path?"

Brian: "Yes, ma'am. My father owns a pool business, and I worked there during the summers. Now that I look back on it, it was an awesome experience overall, but I wasn't so crazy about the menial labor part of it at the time. I started off doing grunt work, scraping gum off chairs and scrubbing the inside of pools. But I worked my way into repairs and noticed that I had a knack for fixing problems and re-designing slides to be safer."

Ms. Kilgore: "I see that you worked for Darnden Hotels. How did you get that job?"

Brian: "I applied at Darnden because I knew I did not want to take over the family business. You see, I like to travel, and I knew that running a pool business would keep me home, tied to the business. With Darnden, I traveled from hotel to hotel testing out slides, examining and fixing pump systems, and figuring how to make slides fun, yet very safe. And well, now I'm here!"

Ms. Kilgore *(smiling)*: "Yes, you are! And you have some unique skills. So, tell me, how did you like working for your father?"

Brian: "Actually, Ms. Kilgore, my dad fired me. I was not such a good employee. I was young, immature, and didn't take it seriously. I missed a lot of work and when I did go in, I was always late. I understand now how unprofessional I was."

Ms. Kilgore: "It's often hard to mix family with business. And we are sort of self-involved as teenagers, aren't we? So, are you still willing to travel frequently if you are hired?"

Brian: "I'm not only willing, but I am dying to travel around. Part of the reason I love what I do is because I get to see the world! I've been to twenty-nine states and several countries. I love seeing the world. I love working outdoors. And I take pride in knowing I'm keeping people safe while they're having fun."

Ms. Kilgore: "I see. What are your long-term goals regarding your career?"

Brian: "I would like to earn a degree in engineering. Hopefully, that would qualify me to get in on the design end of water slides. When I finished high school, I took the opportunity with Darnden and didn't give college much thought. But I know a degree will help me go further in a company like JEG or any other company."

Ms. Kilgore: "Do you realize that Jonathan Entertainment Group has a very generous tuition assistance program for employees who desire to go back to school?"

Brian: "Yes, ma'am, I knew the company offered that. That would be a wonderful benefit for someone like me."

I knew that but didn't want to bring it up; it would have sounded like I just want to work there to further my own agenda, you know?

Ms. Kilgore: "Well, Brian, that's all I have for you right now in this preliminary interview. Do you have any questions for me?"

Brian: "No ma'am…except, when should I expect to hear from you?"

Ms. Kilgore: "You are actually my last interviewee. I'll be speaking soon to our safety manager, John Briggs, about the candidates. We'll decide who we'd like to bring back for a second interview. I'll contact you by phone if you are selected."

Brian: "Thank you so much. I would love to work for Jonathan Entertainment Group, and I hope you'll give me the opportunity to meet with Mr. Briggs. We can talk slides!"

They told me in my interview class to reinforce my desire to work there…so I did it!

Ms. Kilgore *(laughing)*: "He'll like that! Thanks for coming in. Good bye!"

After the Interview

Why do I feel like I just got run over by a truck? I guess I really want this job. I mean, how many water slide tester positions are out there? I lucked into finding out about this one. Plus, those benefits would be awesome!

Other than the music thing, he appears to be a mature young man with the kind of experience we need. I was glad to hear that he realizes how immature he was while working with his father and has learned from his mistakes. Yes, I had an overall good impression!

Would You Give Brian a Second Interview?

❒ Yes, Brian has experience, is willing to travel, and is enthusiastic about the job. He also has ambition and hopes to further his education and job prospects.

❒ No, Brian showed his immaturity by bringing his iPod into the reception area, and he was fired by his father for being unreliable. Is he mature enough to handle a job where he will work at customer sites with no supervision?

Would You Hire This Person?

❒ Yes...because ______________________________

❒ No...because ______________________________

What the Interviewer Decided:

After speaking to Mr. Briggs about Brian, Ms. Kilgore brought Brian in for a second interview. Mr. Briggs liked Brian and was pleased with his experience, but was unsure about sending him to customer sites right away. He and Ms. Kilgore decided to hire Brian, but assign him to a position at JEG's offices for six to nine months to train him and observe his work habits. In four months, Brian had proven himself and was assigned to Wicked Wet Water Park in Australia.

There is nothing wrong with being fired.— Ted Turner

Be Yourself-Not Self-Conscious!

Job candidates are often self-conscious about personal appearance.

Will the job candidate ruin his chances because he's worried about his braces?

Will the interviewer put him at ease…or make it worse?

Will she hire this person?

Would you?

Meet Donna Chang, human resources manager for Tarack Technologies, a research company in the cell phone industry. She is seeking a recent college graduate to fill a network administrator position in the company's IT department. The job will be a bit stressful, and she is looking for a confident team player.

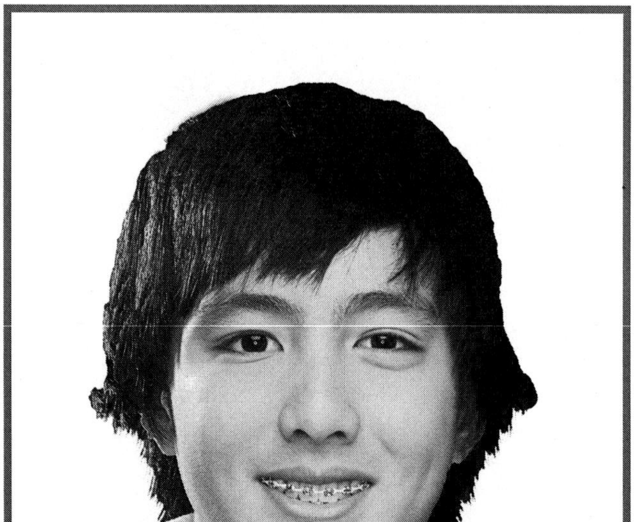

Meet Daniel Ralston. Dan graduated from college four months ago with a Management Information Systems (MIS) degree and is on the hunt for a job. He has good grades, great recommendations, and a solid resume. Why hasn't he landed a job? He suspects that something is holding him back from getting hired—and fears it is the braces on his teeth. When will they go away? Grrrr!

The Interview

Donna Chang sighs and looks at her watch. She only has one more interview today, thank goodness! She just can't seem to find the right fit for the IT job. She pushes back her chair and heads for the reception area just outside her office, where her final candidate awaits his interview.

Ms. Chang: "Dan Ralston?"

Dan *(standing up immediately)*: "Yes, ma'am, that's me."

Ms. Chang: "Great to meet you. Come on in and let's get started. (*She looks closer at him and laughs.*) You won't believe this, but I just bought that same tie for my husband this weekend!"

Dan *(smiling but not showing his teeth)*: "You must have the same taste as my mom. She bought this for me—you know, my good luck red interview tie."

Ms. Chang: "Every man needs one! So, tell me why you have chosen to interview with Tarack Technologies."

Dan: "Well, Ms. Chang, I'm really interested in wireless technology. Cell phones have changed the world, you know, and I would like to be involved in the industry. I know Tarack is involved in many of the innovations in the industry. I think it's a great company."

Ms. Chang: "Why did you choose MIS as your major at Ohio State University? What got you interested in that field? And by the way, I graduated from Ohio State too. Go Buckeyes!"

Dan *(smiling again, but with lips closed)*: "That's great you're a Buckeye, too! That's cool! Well, I wasn't sure what I wanted to major in. Quite honestly, I didn't give it much thought in high school. I was busy playing football and hoped to play in college. I got injured in my senior year so that was the end of that. When it came time to choose a major, I talked to lots of people for advice. My uncle suggested I major in MIS in the business school. He said I'd always find work in the field of computers. I'm good at math, I have a knack for computers, and felt like it was a good fit for me. Now that I'm doing it, I really like it."

Ms. Chang: "I see you had an internship at the university. That's a great gig! What did you do exactly?"

Dan: "I shadowed a network administrator and worked with him in his everyday routine. We worked on improving the local area network, and I got a good dose of all the nuts and bolts it takes to operate a network. It was great to work for the university, and the best part was that I spent a lot of time in the athletic department. I even managed to get free football tickets out of it!"

Ms. Chang: "Dan, I just noticed braces on your teeth. I wore them myself when I was about 30 years old. It wasn't fun but I'm so glad I did it! How do you like them?"

Dan: "I hate them, actually! I first had them in middle school and everything was fine. Then, apparently, my jaw grew and my teeth started hitting each other. I had to wait until I was out of college to get things fixed. I hate interviewing in them."

Ms. Chang: "Don't give them a second thought. Really! You'll be glad you did it. Now, how do you feel about working on a team? That's the way we operate here."

Dan: "That's fine with me, Ms. Chang. I like people and I like to collaborate on things. I know lots of people hated group projects in school, but I didn't mind them. I always liked tossing around ideas. And during my internship, I worked with someone else all the time. A team environment is a good fit for me."

Ms. Chang: "That's good. Can you tell me about any leadership experience you have had?"

Dan: "Do you mean in school, or in sports, or maybe at a job?"

Ms. Chang: "Any leadership experience you would like to tell me about is fine."

Dan: "Uh…well…when I was in college, I worked in the bookstore every summer, except for last summer when I had my internship. One of our big jobs was to prepare for the fall rush of textbook buying. After my first year, I had experience, so I trained the new employees every year about how to handle the fall rush. I also became the team leader and 'go to' guy when any problems came up."

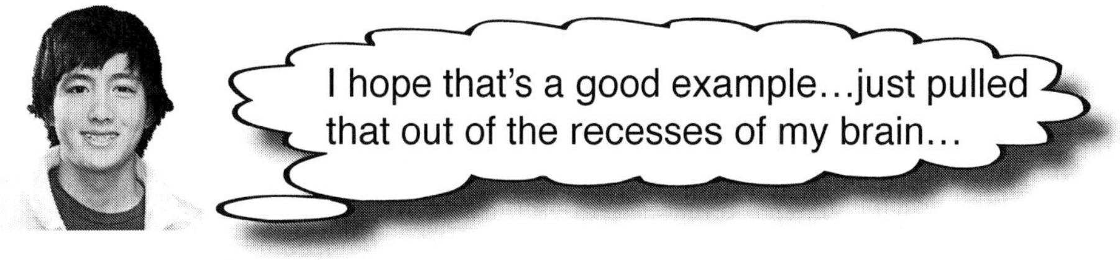

Ms. Chang: "How did you like the added responsibility?"

Dan: "Oh, it was fine. At first, I thought it was going to be a big hassle, but I found if you provide good training in the first place, you have fewer problems in the long run."

Ms. Chang *(smiling and nodding)*: "Yes, that's one of those good life lessons better to learn early on, I would say! Well, Dan, I've really enjoyed meeting you. I'll be discussing the candidates with the IT manager and then we'll call back several people for a second interview. I'll be in touch by e-mail."

Dan *(with a big smile, braces and all)*: "Sounds great! Thank you so much for your time, and I hope to hear from you."

Dan and Ms. Chang exchange goodbyes and Dan heads out to his car.

After the Interview

I felt so comfortable talking to her! It was great to just be myself and not worry about these darn braces. That's it. I'm not going to let them sap my confidence anymore! I need to start selling myself in these interviews.

I like this young man. He certainly came out of his shell after we talked about the braces. His grades are good, and his internship experience will impress the IT department.

Would You Give Dan a Second Interview?

☐ Yes, Dan was reserved at first, but became more confident after the discussion about his braces. His internship experience is a real plus.

☐ No, Dan showed immaturity by being so concerned about his braces. He needs to build his self-confidence before taking on a high-pressure job like this one.

Would You Hire This Person?

☐ Yes…because ____

☐ No…because ____

What the Interviewer Decided:

Ms. Chang and the IT manager reviewed the candidates and decided to bring Dan back for a second interview. From the minute he sat down, Dan displayed confidence and was not afraid of being himself, braces and all. He impressed the IT manager with his knowledge of network operations, and was hired for an entry-level position. Dan got his braces off six months later, got a girlfriend, and got married!

The "Name" of the Game

People forget or mispronounce names all the time.

However, that's not a good thing in a job interview.

Will this job candidate realize her mistake before it's too late?

Will the interviewer hire this person?

Would you?

Meet Rita Jefferson, owner of two consignment stores selling gently used clothing for women and children. She is a no-nonsense entrepreneur who needs a manager to handle the day-to-day operations of her stores. She is looking for a sharp, creative, capable candidate with experience in the retail field.

Meet Amala Nadeer. She has worked in retail stores since she turned 16. She would love to get into management to further her career. She hopes to impress Rita Jefferson, who was recently named "Small Businesswoman of the Year" in Eden Prairie, Minnesota.

The Interview

Amala Nadeer is right on time for her interview at Savvy Styles, one of Rita Jefferson's consignment stores. She waits patiently at the checkout counter while Rita finishes speaking with a customer.

Ms. Jefferson: "Yes, can I help you?"

Amala: "Yes, I am Amala Nadeer. I'm here for an interview with the owner about the management position advertised in the paper."

Ms. Jefferson: "Oh, great! I am the owner, Rita Jefferson. Great to meet you. Pardon the clothes piled up here, but that's what we're all about it, isn't it? Just follow me back to my office."

Amala takes a seat in front of Ms. Jefferson's antique cherry desk. A framed newspaper article with the headline "Rita Jefferson: Small Businesswoman of the Year" stares at Amala from across the desk.

Ms. Jefferson: "So, Amala, tell me about your experience in retail. I see you have worked for a small store and a nationwide department store. They must have been very different experiences."

Amala: "Well, Ms. Jones, I started working in clothing stores when I was in high school just for a part-time job. At first, it was just a job, but then I realized I really liked it. I found I had a knack for creating displays and dressing mannequins in the window to attract people's attention. It became a passion of mine. I got so many compliments on how the store looked!"

Ms. Jefferson: "That's great to hear that you have a fashion eye. That's important in this business, as well. We like to feature up-to-date styles in our front windows to bring customers in. Unfortunately, many people think of consignment stores as having old, stodgy, throwaway items."

Amala: "You're right! So many consignment stores just look awful."

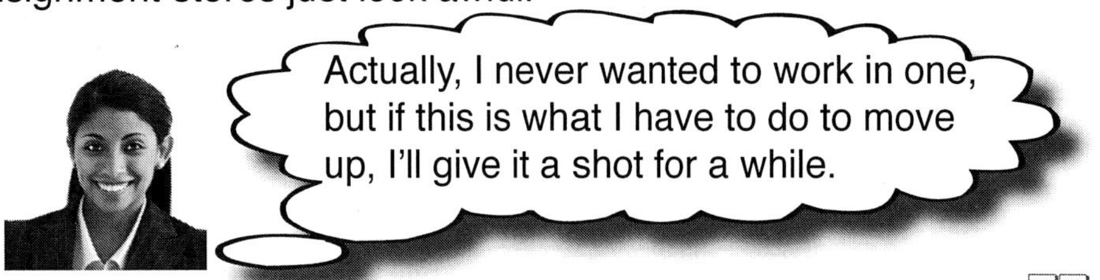

Ms. Jefferson: "What about the business side of things, Amala? What involvement have you had with that?"

Amala: "Do you mean like running the register and handling the money?"

Ms. Jefferson: "Yes, like running the register and handling the money—but much more, like managing inventory and employees?"

Amala: "Oh! Well, Ms. Jones, I did manage inventory in Girl Stop, the first store I worked in—"

Ms. Jefferson: "I'm sorry to interrupt, but my name is Rita Jefferson, not Jones."

Amala: "I'm so sorry! *(laughing)* I'm not that good with names."

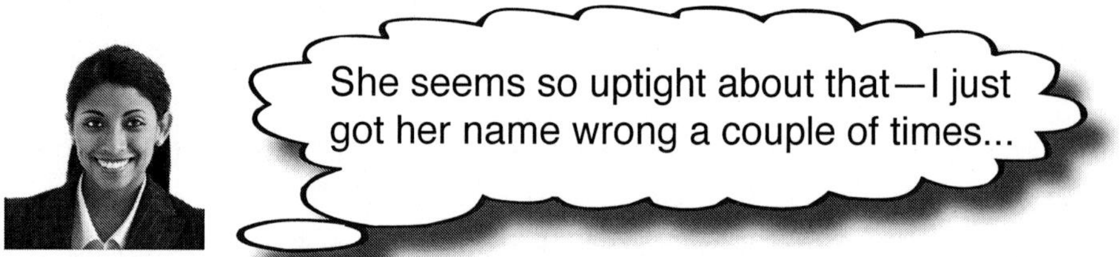

Ms. Jefferson: "I'm sorry to hear that, Amala, because it's very important to remember names in this business. I have many repeat customers and it's important to welcome them every time they enter the store, either to buy things or leave things for consignment."

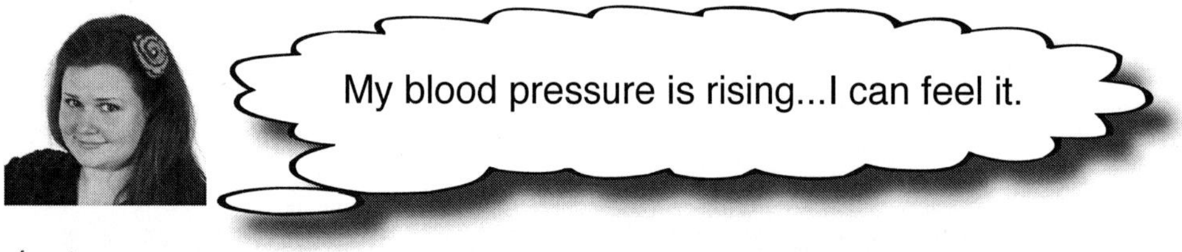

Amala: "Yes, ma'am. I understand. That would be something I would work on very hard."

Ms. Jefferson: "Now, where were we? Yes, you were talking about your time at Girl Stop."

Amala: "Yes. I was very involved in managing inventory and learned a lot about it while I worked there. That's the good thing about a small store. You learn about everything. As for employees, I did not hire and fire people, but I did manage some of the younger girls as I became the senior person there. That took a lot of work and patience, because so many teenagers don't take their job responsibilities seriously at that age."

Ms. Jefferson: "What about your time at Westwood's? What did you take away from that experience with a big department store?"

Amala: "A big store is so different from a small one! There are so many corporate rules and policies to follow. I did not have the freedom I had at Girl Stop for window displays and things like that. I missed that, but I did enjoy the fast pace of it. There were continual deliveries, and things to move around the floor, and things to mark down…it certainly made the time go fast."

Ms. Jefferson: "So why are you interested in managing consignment stores?"

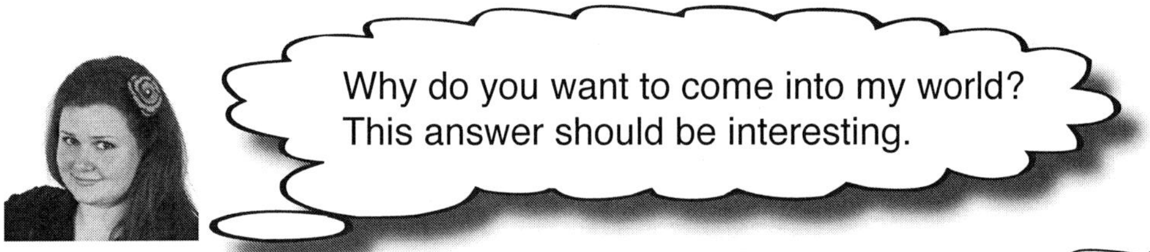

Amala: "First of all, I want to move into management. I really feel I'm ready for that. And second, I thought I could use my creative side here with displays and stuff like that. That's why, really."

Ms. Jefferson: "OK, Amala, it's been great to meet you. I'm discussing all the candidates with my business partner and then we'll decide who we'd like to talk to further. Thank you for coming."

Amala: "Thank you, Ms. Jones…I mean, Ms. Jefferson. I'm so sorry! Names…got to work on that!" *Amala giggles in embarrassment as she heads for the door.*

After the Interview

I hope I haven't totally blown it by calling her the wrong name! But she didn't need to get so uptight about it! She's kind of hard-edged, might be kind of hard to work for, you know?

Yes, she has experience in retail. However, mess up my name once and I can deal with it. But three times? Come on! This is not high school, this is business—my business!

Would You Give Amala a Second Interview?

❒ Yes, Amala is quite creative, and has solid retail experience. She may have made a mistake with Ms. Jefferson's name, but she can work on that.

❒ No, mixing up your interviewer's name three times is a bad sign. It shows inattention to detail and disrespect. In addition, Amala did not show much enthusiasm for Rita Jefferson's consignment business.

Would You Hire This Person?

❒ Yes...because ____

❒ No...because ____

What the Interviewer Decided:

Rita Jefferson did not invite Amala Nadeer back to meet her business partner. She was annoyed by Amala's mistakes with her name and dismayed that Amala didn't have a positive reason for wanting to manage the consignment stores. Her reasons for wanting the job were "all about Amala," not about the business. Amala went on to bomb out with six more interviews, then she went back to school!

Tips to ACE Your Next Job Interview

You know, it's not required that you are a nervous wreck for a job interview!

Prep ahead and be prepared—your possible boss will be...impressed!

1. **Do your due diligence**. Find out all you can about the company you're interviewing with, their industry, and the position you're interviewing for.
2. **Role play.** Practice giving answers out loud before your interview. This can help you fine-tune what you're going to say and wean the jitters out of your voice.
3. **Dress to impress.** You never get a second chance to make a first impression. Dress appropriately, give a firm handshake, use direct eye contact, and speak confidently (even if you are nervous!).
4. **Be on time!** Period.
5. **Be prepared with answers to even tough questions.** No matter what the question, share short, sweet, pre-thought-out answers with honesty, enthusiasm, and confidence.
6. **Have a good attitude.** Skills may get you an interview, but attitude determines whether you'll get an offer.
7. **Be prepared to explain employment gaps.** "So…why didn't this kid ever work a summer job?" the interviewer may wonder. Be prepared to volunteer an outstanding explanation (if you have one) whether asked or not. Don't be shy. If you helped take care of your aunt in hospice one summer, well, that's a highly mature, respectable, responsible thing and probably nets you more points than a fast food gig. Be proud, not embarrassed or reticent to share your other "I really was working" situations.
8. **Know your strengths AND weaknesses.** It's easy to talk about the things you do well. But if asked to talk about something you haven't yet aced, be prepared to tell how you're overcoming that weakness.
9. **Give examples.** Be prepared to give specific examples in your work or school history. One good story that demonstrates your skill level or talent is worth more than simply saying you have that skill.

10. **Don't be negative!** Even if you are asked, "Who was your worst teacher/boss/manager?", don't fall into the negative trap. Answer: "My toughest teacher really challenged me, but taught me that I could allow myself to excel beyond my expectations."

11. **Know where you want to go.** A common question interviewers ask is "Where do you see yourself in five years?" Don't say "Hawaii!"...just be prepared to give a short answer: "I'd like to excel at this job so that I could either move into a supervisory or training role. I'd also like to work at one of your international branches."

12. **Listen.** Don't be so self-involved or talk too long that you miss important cues the interviewer may give you, such as what type of employee they are looking for or what personality would be the best fit in their company.

13. **Ask questions.** The questions you ask the interviewer show how interested you really are in the job and in the business. Examples: "How would you describe the work culture here?" "How have the recent industry changes affected the company?" "What is the most important attribute you look for in an employee?" A first interview is NOT the time to ask about salary or money!

14. **It's not about YOU!** Really! All of your answers must say what you can do for *them*, and how you can help *them*...the questions aren't really about *you* at all!

15. **Follow up and say "thank you."** Always follow up with the interviewer by writing a short letter thanking them for their time and the opportunity to interview.

Let's see, I think I said "prepare or be prepared" a lot in these tips, hint, hint!

So many people out there have no idea what they want to do for a living, but they think that by going on job interviews they'll magically figure it out. If you're not sure, that message comes out loud and clear in the interview.—Todd Bermont

FOR MIDDLE SCHOOL, HIGH SCHOOL, COLLEGE AND **BEYOND!**

"If you are ready for 'readiness'...for choosing a career pathway... deciding what to do after high school...or for a first job, or raise and promotion - THIS SERIES IS FOR YOU!"

– James Barnard

Job Tracks: 60* Great Careers and How to Get from Where You Are... to Where You Want To Go!

This book is filled with unique and effective approaches for helping students find their career pathway! Featuring 60 careers from today's job market, this book allows young people to hear first-hand from a person with the job: how they got it, what they do, what education and skills were required, and "what I would have done differently!" Readers get the feel of what particular careers might actually be like—essential knowledge for that all-important decision!

"Entertaining and charming to read!"

Essential Skills for the Real World of Work: Things EVERY Student Must Know!

There's no other book that does a better job of sharing essential skills for the real business world and explaining why they are essential! This book dishes out the subtleties, nuances, and in-between-the-lines considerations of job interviewers who are not only interested in candidates with essential skills, but are actually desperate for them! It includes a fun and effective scoring system to encourage students to rack up job-readiness skills long before they are required.

"Highly encouraging and enlightening!"

Would You Hire This Person? A Look at Getting Hired (or Not!)...from the Point of View of Your (Possible!) Future Employer

Read verbatim interviews that are both entertaining and enlightening! In this book, students hear both sides of the interview, including the employer and job candidate's unspoken thoughts. The reader can decide for himself or herself if they would hire the job candidate before learning the actual outcome.

"Such realistic scenarios – I got nervous reading them! I wanted the person to get the job, but, gee...I can see why some would not!"

www.careerscurriculum.com

Work Words: Job/Business/Career Words & Terms You Need to Know!

Get ready for lots of insider information and a few inside jokes! Written by a real employer, this book defines essential job, business, and career words and terms with insight, humor, and pizzazz! The contents of the book are organized into entertaining and effective groupings.

"Why be embarrassed when you can be empowered by knowing 'job speak' BEFORE you even get the job?"

Business Ethics & Etiquette for Students: You MUST Know These!

This highly entertaining and immensely practical book is an eye-opening must-read for students and new hires! It provides them with the confidence to avoid embarrassment, misstep, lost opportunity, and more.

"Fascinating and quite a lot of material covered. Anyone can benefit from this double-whammy of info book!"

The Parent and Teacher's Guide: Helping Students Navigate the Bumpy Road from School to More School, First Job, and Career

Filled with candid help from someone who has traveled the bumpy road of "non-readiness" from school to job to career, this book boasts timely and honest information that will help kids get ready for the real world of work. The wealth of ideas available to parents and teachers in this book will help them to navigate their student's journey ahead!

"Marsh has a keen sense of devotion to every type of student truly seeking a path to success. This book is worth the price for the compassion and humor, explanation of 'Rigor vs. Rigor Mortis,' and 'Why Study These Subjects' section. She's clearly 'been there, done that,' and achieved great success despite many obstacles!"

Carole Marsh's CAREERS CURRICULUM™

PLEASE CONTINUE TO VISIT OUR WEBSITE FOR MORE K-12 PRODUCTS IN PRINT & ONLINE FORMATS, INCLUDING:

- INDIVIDUAL CAREER MANUAL
- SCHOOL INFORMATION SHEETS
- COMPANY PROFILE SHEETS
- MAP OF OPPORTUNITIES
- ESSENTIAL SKILLS PASSPORT BOOK
- ... AND MUCH MORE!!

FOR MIDDLE SCHOOL, HIGH SCHOOL, COLLEGE AND **BEYOND!**

www.careerscurriculum.com